The Wicked Six

BY SHO OKUMOTO

By the same author, you can purchase other books of his through Amazon through this link here:

https://www.amazon.com/author/shookumoto

-For my mother

-This book is a work of fiction. Names, characters, places, and incidents either are products of the author's imagination or are used fictitiously.

Description

The Wicked Six is an exciting fun book, filled with inspirational six-word quotes plus six-word stories.

It is an easy, quick, fun read, guarantee to put a smile on your face.

The Wicked Six

1- Open mind, learn, and achieve greatness.

2- Enjoy life, enjoy every moment passionately.

3- Killer vanished mysteriously.   Wrong person, captured.

4- Stop being serious.   Just enjoy life.

5- Positive vibes, positive atmosphere, brings happiness.

6- Cat on a tree, escaping water.

7- Special delivery, a letter, an opportunity.

8- Upset, empty stomach.   Food brings happiness.

9- Deliver the goods, I deliver dollars.

10- Robbing a bank, arrested, serving time.

11- Sunrise, smile, new day, new start.

12- There is no tomorrow.   Start today.

13- Life is short.   Go live fully.

14- Shoot fast, to survive another massacre.

15- Eating spinach.   Didn't work.   Protein shake.

16- Plant knowledge.   Physically experience the truth.

17- Play with creativity to create greatness.

18- Drinking beer, relaxed, confident, new date.

19- Flash of light, sprinted, police coming.

20- At court pleaded guilty.   Penalty paid.

21- Drinking fast, no alcohol, wallet empty.

22- Books are great.   Entering fantasy world.

23- Beers, bacon, short life, so what.

24- Poker, bad hand, bluff, I won.

25- Trying to get a date. Rejected.

26- Sad days bring happy days.   Believe.

27- Hate work.   Take risks.   Be adventurous.

28- The teacher teaching math.   I slept.

29- Movie, fried chicken, beer, my night.

30- Drag race.   Adrenaline-fueled entertainment for petrolheads.

31- Eating raw oysters.   My heavenly place.

32- Beer goggles on, making bad decisions.

33- Living fast, criminal records, no future.

34- Rob the rich.   Sell the valuables.

35- Fast trip.   Still late to work.

36- Switching channels, bored, reading a book.

37- Working overtime, shit pay, miserable life.

38- Be bold, be determined.   Go succeed.

39- Chefs all start by washing dishes.

40- Teaching is a skill.   Equals perfectionist.

41- Summer, barbeque time, friends, great
atmosphere.

42- Love life, life will love you.

43- Win smartly or lose badly.   Decision-making.

44- Youth, big ego.   Age defeats idiots.

45- Think fast to escape prison time.

46- A disloyal junky owes me money.

47- Pushing pen all day, brain fried.

48- Smacked into a car.   Keep driving.

49- Boring day, creative storytelling to entertain.

50- Select words wisely to prevent arguments.

51- Killing the demon kills negative thoughts.

52- Think wild, be wild, party time.

53- Criminal once.   Writing a crime book.

54- Don't get discouraged.   Your work rocks.

55- Don't destroy masterpieces.   Embrace everyone's creativity.

56- Dream big, capture it.   Succeed big.

57- Be free to dream.   Capture it.

58- Cry, repair, recover.   Now, go achieve.

59- Bright light, bright soul, positive energy.

60- Live to learn.   Die in peace.

61- Shy once.   Writing gave me confidence.

62- So what.   Move on with life.

63- I surrender.   Let me live, please.

64- Got bullied.   Stood up.   Fought back.

65- Too expensive?   Piss off.   We're quality.

66- Appreciate every day.   Life is precious.

67- Work hard to build your dream.

68- Fear nothing.   Believe.   Keep pushing forward.

69- After work drinks.   Heavy drinking.   Hungover.

70- Enjoy creating.   Have fun.   No pressure.

71- Stoned.   Not lazy.   Just hate work.

72- Selling my watch to buy presents.

73- Horse betting, lost all my money.

74- Tough love builds strength.   Stronger bond.

75- Take time.   Drain negativity.   Bring peace.

76- Taking a bubble bath.   Champagne.   Relaxed.

77- A chef must study knife skills.

78- Spreading positivity.   The world becomes happy.

79- Sprinting.   Train doors closing.   Train gone.

80- Fast life.   You miss life moments.

81- Business meeting.   Fell asleep.   In trouble.

82- Shooting stars.   We fly through dreams.

83- Martial arts are powerful.   Be humble.

84- Killed a gangster.   Framed the rat.

85- Guns kill quickly.   Knives are personal.

86- Boss has money.   Doesn't pay staff.

87- Seeing butterflies.   Are messages of happiness.

88- No drugs.   Steal.   Sell.   Getting high.

89- The library.   My comfort.   Escaping hell.

90- Toilet blocked.   Plunging away.   Brown surprise.

91- Starving, skinny as a pencil, homeless.

92- Evil shooter.   The lions got him.

93- Mosh pit, going insane.   Nostalgic band.

94- Classics never die.   They keep rocking.

95- Gunna fly to space.   Completely wasted.

96- Exhausted from work.   Microwaving processed food.

97- Become a kid.   Free the mind.

98- Christmas tree, family, great moments. Happiness.

99- Nostalgia train.   Go relive the past.

100- The key to success.   Believe confidently.

101- Time defeats people.   Never give up.

102- Smile at failures.   Learn to triumph.

103- Quit, no results.   Keep going confidently.

104- Expensive petrol.   EV is the future.

105- Technology.   Spoon-fed future.   Never forget skills.

106- Gym builds muscles.   Imagination creates creativity.

107- Cooking steak, toilet rush, burnt meal.

108- Start.   Stay busy, opportunities will come.

109- People need entertainment.   Share your masterpieces.

110- Big dreams.   Big goals.   Big success.

111- Found cash.   A woman leaving.   Thinking.

112- Midnight train to my magical dreams.

113- Intelligence defeats physical abilities.   Compete wisely.

114- Blood dripping from above.   Vampires everywhere.

115- Real love?   I got used.   Idiot.

116- Burnt toast.   Bad start, still hungover.

117- Kids walking.   Cars slowing down safely.

118- Christmas summer at the beach.   Perfect.

119- Stars are dreams.   Go capture it.

120- Experiences come from life.   Keep exploring.

121- Cashier staring.   Dammit.   Forgot my ID.

122- Underage, using a fake ID, worked.

123- Cashier staring, fake ID not working.

124- Powerful car, bad driver, lost control.

125- Early morning.   Sipping coffee, I'm ready.

126- Passed the exit, handbrake, going back.

127- The art of creativity is self-expression.

128- Salty food.   I need a beer.

129- Washed car.   Cat lands, marking everywhere.

130- Playing an instrument.   Bad crowd.   Booed.

131- Open mind.   Simple plans.   Living life.

132- Smelling success, means you're getting closer.

133- I'm the superhero in my world.

134- One life, one chance, go hard.

135- Stupid decisions.   Cops are watching.   Careful.

136- A bird singing.   Another magnificent morning.

137- See the truth.   Real stories appear.

138- In tough times, we appreciate life.

139- A great career is your passion.

140- Discover yourself to understand yourself deeply.

141- Your productivity, determines your true results.

142- Knowledge is power.   Action is results.

143- Toro tuna.   Sake.   Time for sashimi.

144- Celebration dance.   Finally, a pay rise.

145- Fishing.   Nothing.   Time for a beer.

146- Don't ruin yourself because of stupidity.

147- The car keeps stalling.   It's manual.

148- Parasites are disloyal people.   Backstabbing bastards.

149- Surf the wind toward life beauties.

150- Opportunities are everywhere.   Just gotta explore.

151- Dive underwater to a magical world.

152- Potato couch, flicking channels, no future.

153- Dinner party.   Selfish.   Lasagna is mine.

154- Watched a gangster movie.   I'm bulletproof.

155- Travel the world to experience life.

156- Drinking juice at the pub.   Outsider.

157- Shopping madness.   Time to steal goods.

158- Sakura blossoming, spring awakening, hanami time.

159- Big waves, paddling out, surf on.

160- Ego limits you.   Lose the ego.

161- Creativity is the freedom to express.

162- Plant creativity, to blossom your masterpieces.

163- Hate news.   Shows my true intelligence.

164- Small or big project.   Finish it.

165- Storytelling is a maze.   Entertains audiences.

166- Jealous people are your biggest haters.

167- Some find success early.   Some later.

168- Don't dictate life.   Live life freely.

169- Don't question the future.   Just ride.

170- Drunk.   Taking a leak.   Pissing non-stop.

171- Lake.   Kayaking.   Rippling waters.   Mysterious creature.

172- Teacher's tedious speech.   Slowly dozing off.

173- Flat tire.   One spare, no jack.

174- Stop worrying.   Let the worrying go.

175- Always move forward.   Never go backward.

176- Your dreams will flourish.   Keep believing

177- Enjoy your age.   All great experiences.

178- Overthinking will make you struggle.   Breathe.

179- Gave a corsage.   Magical night.   Prom.

180- Waving.   The taxi drove past.   Wanker.

181- Fly high, touch greatness.   Keep going.

182- Window shopping.   Everything is ridiculously expensive.

183- Desires or essentials.   Money tight.
Pondering.

184- Traffic.   Cutting cars off.   I'm late.

185- Beach bodies everywhere.   My beer gut.

186- Crashed dad's car.   Blaming someone else.

187- First interview.   Nervous, stuttering.   Good
results.

188- Megaproject.   Planning, organizing.   Finally,
started construction.

189- A quick catch-up.   Still an asshole.

190- Annoying salesperson convinced me to buy.

191- People downloading MP3.   I'm buying CDs.

192- Positive aggression, focus, achieve great
success.

193- One person can change your life.

194- Gift kindness, to bring positive light.

195- Produce quality craftsmanship to showcase magic.

196- Photos never age but we do.

197- Photos is our greatest time machine.

198- To fake a cry.   Cut onions.

199- Release the past.   Discover the new.

200- Express your emotions, to craft masterpieces.

201- Comedy is a great stress buster.

202- Fussy cat wants different meals regularly.

203- Camping.   Bonfire.   Daydreaming.   Cooking marshmallow.   Liquefied.

204- Create with love to create awesomeness.

205- Fight to survive.   Leave to live.

206- Exit your dream to enter reality.

207- Happiness starts from you.   Be positive.

208- Quickest escape is to conquer goals.

209- Approaching your situation determines true results.

210- Your happiness will spread positive vibes.

211- Happy life, big future.   Be ready.

212- Learn to survive the street environment.

213- No money, no food.   Think smarter.

214- Connections are important.   Build good relationships.

215- Think fast to win the argument.

216- Snoozing is not losing.   Just bored.

217- Don't hate the winner.   Beat them.

218- Hate is harsh.   Dislike is better.

219- No money.   Sell art.   Poker time.

220- Heavy foot, adrenaline pumping, drag racing.

221- Illuminations will lure and hypnotize people.

222- Ideas need action to become reality.

223- Self-expression creates a powerful unique masterpiece.

224- Confidence is believing in your actions.

225- Be the comic to spread elation.

226- To grow, keep learning, keep experiencing.

227- Few drinks, bulletproof confidence, speech time.

228- Too many drinks, I become foolish.

229- Gaming is a utopia.   Entertaining players.

230- Sniffing the white snow, party junky.

231- Go beyond your potential.   No limits.

232- Laughter gives happiness to fatigued hearts.

233- Heaven gave us life.   Appreciate life.

234- Sit back.   Enjoy the life ride.

235- Wake up positively to delete negativity.

236- I suck at rugby.   Damn, butterfingers.

237- Independence gives you freedom of choice.

238- Stopped smoking but I love whiskey.

239- I drink to enjoy.   Deleting stress.

240- There is no wrong.   Just uniqueness.

241- White feather floating.   Miracles are coming.

242- Witness the beauty of nature daily.

243- Riding horses.   A pure, magical feeling.

244- Your actions determine your true
characteristics.

245- Experiencing failures teach you to appreciate.

246- Suffer now.   Patience.   Success will come.

247- Life is mysterious.   Filled with surprises.

248- Capture creativity.   Opportunity to create gold.

249- Repetition is the key to success.

250- Money is temporary happiness.   Find happiness.

251- Shit day.   Sun rises, start again.

252- Share positive ideas to inspire everyone.

253- Capture love and happiness.   Spread positivity.

254- Fatigue sucks.   But keep moving forward.

255- Be bold, be confident.   Keep believing.

256- Lie convincingly to escape prison time.

257- The world is updating.   Keep learning.

258- Stay ready.   Be ready to fight.

259- Our childhood dreams are our passion.

260- Music is our timeline of memories.

261- Pets fill our emptiness.   Unconditional love.

262- Violence solves nothing.   Peace solves everything.

263- The system sucks.   Create your system.

264- Investigating multiple homicides.   Linked. Family crime.

265- Target missed.   Accidentally shot my car.

266- Murder.   Created by a crafty author.

267- Taking over the family business.   Crumbled.

268- Prisoners read books.   Finally got released.

269- Ran for miles.   Emptying my thoughts.

270- Partying with the devil.   Breaking rules.

271- Crime novel.   Author writing their confessions.

272- Men thinking with their sausage, cheat.

273- Escaping prison time.   Like dodging bullets.

274- Strict parents, rebellious kids, causing mayhem.

275- Loud banging sound.   Cops are here.

276- Change is great.   Stay on track.

277- Staff toilet.   Farted.   Heard laughter.
Embarrassed.

278- Hard work beats talent.   Keep going.

279- Don't let negativity enter your passion.

280- I am not afraid.   Live fully.

281- Use your experiences to inspire people.

282- Performing a show.   Audiences falling asleep.

283- I ate anger.   Spat out happiness.

284- I am complicated.   People are idiots.

285- Nature is love.   Work is pain.

286- Hard work and perseverance create
opportunities.

287- Creativity is freedom.   Free your mind.

288- Yellow traffic light.   Accelerator pedal down.

289- Delete the hate to show love.

290- Express emotions to create to share.

291- Idiots running the country.   We're screwed.

292- Speak the truth.   Get honest answers.

293- I hate politics.   I love sports.

294- Support your stories.   Stories support you.

295- Happiness gives you peace.   Enjoy life.

296- Salt and pepper.   True unconditional love.

297- One hit wonder.   I am happy.

298- Good decisions.   Positive journey.   Positive life.

299- Enjoy your journey.   Never forget that.

300- Confidence is personal belief.   Conquer life.

301- Belief in dreams.   Experience the adventure.

302- You are your kryptonite.   Be careful.

303- Transform yourself into the best you.

304- Leave the past.   Change the future.

305- Arguments create mayhem.   Peace solves everything.

306- Writing a story.   Dreams become reality.

307- Free your mind to live free.

308- Belief in yourself.   Fail.   Rise.   Continue.

309- Our senses are our memories.   Nostalgia.

310- Learn to unwind.   Release, relax.   Refresh.

311- Understand your dreams.   Create your reality.

312- Dreams are your reality.   Take action.

313- Become your psychologist.   Truly understand yourself.

314- Lies escape to reveal the truth.

315- No guns.   Spies negotiate, using cheques.

316- Secret agent.   Three-digit code name.   Elite.

317- Technology fails.   Knowledge.   Skills become useful.

318- Some cheat.   Stay genuine to achieve.

319- Fake people destroy lives.   Be cautious.

320- Feeling dreams are fading?   Keep manifesting.

321- Remember.   Keep believing and dream big.

322- Whatever happens, stay humble.   Be positive.

323- Understand the reality and move on.

324- No ambitions, the less you explore.

325- Goals.   The purpose of exploring life.

326- Don't run away.   Face reality confidently.

327- Strength comes from a calm mind.

328- Key to survival.   Learn from locals.

329- Every job is difficult.   Don't judge.

330- Positive input.   Always achieve positive results.

331- Library, my comfort world.   My escape.

332- Keep manifesting.   Bring dreams into reality.

333- Burnt out.   No flame, no desire.

334- Drinking alcohol, creativity starts to flow.

335- Drink happily to write.   Edit sober.

336- Machines will take over.   Stealing jobs.

337- We'll become dumber as technology progresses.

338- Free your mind.   Free your creativity.

339- Never be afraid.   Just be yourself.

340- Thrash metal, adrenaline pumping.   Rock show.

341- Leave crime.   Become a good person.

342- Life choices are everywhere.   Choose wisely.

343- When creating, be unique.   Express yourself.

344- Don't think small.   Always believe big.

345- Leaving the past is difficult.   Memories.

346- Money is not everything.   Love unconditionally.

347- Learn to fly.   Fly to succeed.

348- Failure is a lesson.   Don't repeat.

349- I've cried.   I've recovered.   I'm ready.

350- Didn't work.   Keep finding a way.

351- Your creativity is magic.   Always believe.

352- Shootout.   Dodging bullets.   Escaping the

massacre.

353- Cherish every moment before it ends.

354- To release stress, I write stories.

355- Open the window.   Let potential flow.

356- Timing is everything.   We will succeed.

357- We will fail.   We will succeed.

358- Belief in life.   Everything is achievable.

359- We are all born with creativity.

360- Flexibility in creativity, you become unique.

361- A touch is a powerful message.

362- We are philosophers of our life.

363- A detective speaking freely, got murdered.

364- Ranked highly, quits job, bottom again.

365- Unplug from reality.   Enjoy your dreams.

366- Corruption is the enemy.   Must destroy.

367- Nothing is real.   We create reality.

368- Trapped in reality.   Dreams are freedom.

369- We are machines controlled by corruption.

370- Time ticking away.   Cherish life moments.

371- Many great artists are lonely people.

372- Orchestrate your creativity to produce brilliance.

373- Keep manifesting.   Keep believing.   Be productive.

374- One shot.   Turn dreams into reality.

375- Complaining.   No results.   Just work hard.

376- Talking is simple.   Emotions are deeper.

377- Nothing is guaranteed.   Gotta capture it.

378- Genuinely believe.   Bring dreams to life.

379- Create from your heart.   Be unique.

380- Emotions are stories, expressing your experiences.

381- Some mature quickly.   Some mature slower.

382- Comfort, no success.   Risk to succeed.

383- Jealous people are haters.   Mute them.

384- Stop stressing.   Relax.   Live.   Be positive.

385- Money is no apology.   Heart is.

386- Fast is good.   But be efficient.

387- Too many shoes.   Wasted my money.

388- Addicted to hobbies.   Better than drugs.

389- Friends.   Drinking beers.   Watching boxing. Awesomeness.

390- Peanut butter, jam sandwich.   Drooling hungrily.

391- Work hard to enjoy life freely.

392- Hate working, love playing.   Retire early.

393- No bottle opener.   Using my teeth.

394- Dentist is expensive.   DIY at home.

395- Live fast, grow old and retire.

396- Editing is a wave.   Tough process.

397- Gambling.   Pissing millions away.   Stupid boy.

398- Delicious food.   Stomach full.   Happy day.

399- Capture excitement, capture brilliance.   Go create.

400- Love.   Keep loving unconditionally.   Connect forever.

401- Don't be afraid.   Just keep going.

402- Spew your creativity out to produce.

403- Love your life.   Happily, love yourself.

404- Golf sucks.   A cooler filled.   Beers.

405- Deep in the underworld.   No escape.

406- Biggest criminals are the corrupt cops.

407- Good detectives, play bad for information.

408- Lost souls commit crimes, joining gangs.

409- Sadness is important.   Part of life.

410- Mind for visions.   Hands for creating.

411- Everyone loves the beach.   It's peaceful.

412- Cook wonderful food to spread happiness.

413- Being positive can be tough.   Try.

414- Creativity is an escape.   Express yourself.

415- Dreams are born when we're kids.

416- Without confidence, we're dead.   Be confident.

417- Eat happily.   Live a long life.

418- We all have potential.   Find it.

419- Walk alone toward your passionate dreams.

420- When you create, create something addictive.

421- Heavy bass, guitar solo, rock hard.

422- Passion gives us words to express.

423- Build yourself to become a successor.

424- Become a legend.   Become unforgettable.
Believe.

425- Make masterpieces for people to escape.

426- Find your passion.   Build your dream.

427- Drinking gives me creativity.   Dammit.
Overtime.

428- Slowing the brain to relax.   Impossible.

429- Failed many times.   Achieved my dreams.

430- Feeling fear is normal.   Be confident.

431- We have a purpose.   To succeed.

432- Be unique, be seen.   Become successful.

433- Music is our nostalgia.   Great memories.

434- We will reach our potential.   Believe.

435- Become better than potential.   Become
awesome.

436- Drinking to success.   It is rewarding.

437- The Wicked Six.   Six-word entertainment.
Thanks.